THROUGH
ARTISTS' EYES

War &
Conflict

Jane Bingham

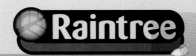

www.raintreepublishers.co.uk
Visit our website to find out more information about **Raintree** books.

To order:
☎ Phone 44 (0) 1865 888113
🖹 Send a fax to 44 (0) 1865 314091
🖥 Visit the Raintree bookshop at **www.raintreepublishers.co.uk** to browse our catalogue and order online.

First published in Great Britain by Raintree,
Halley Court, Jordan Hill, Oxford OX2 8EJ,
part of Harcourt Education.

Raintree is a registered trademark of Harcourt Education Ltd.

Editorial: Isabel Thomas and Rosie Gordon
Design: Richard Parker & Tinstar Design www.tinstar.com
Picture Research: Hannah Taylor and Zoe Spilberg
Production: Duncan Gilbert

Originated by Chroma Graphics
Printed and bound in China by South China Printing Company

10-digit ISBN 1 406 20149 9
13-digit ISBN 978 1 4062 0149 9

10 09 08 07 06
10 9 8 7 6 5 4 3 2 1

British Library Cataloguing in Publication Data
Bingham, Jane
   War and conflict. - (Through artists' eyes)
   1.War in art - Juvenile literature 2.Art - History -
   Juvenile literature
   I.Title
                  704.9'49303485

The publishers would like to thank Karen Hosack for her assistance in the preparation of this book.

Acknowledgements
The publishers would like to thank the following for permission to reproduce photographs: **p. 19**, © 1990, Photo Scala, Florence/ Bayeux Museum; **p. 30**, © 1990, Photo Scala, Florence/ Prado, Madrid; **p. 25**, © 2005, Photo Smithsonian American Art Museum/ Art Resource/ Scala, Florence; **p. 38**, © DACS 2006 Photo: ©2004, Photo The Philadelphia Museum of Art/ Art Resource/ Scala, Florence; **pp. 40-41**, © Succession Picasso/ DACS 2006 Photo: ©2003, Photo Art Resource/ Scala, Florence/ John Bigelow Taylor; **p. 51**, © Succession Picasso/ DACS 2006 Photo: Bridgeman Art Library/ Private Collection, Archives Charmet; **p. 11**, Ancient Art and Architecture Collection Ltd/ C.M. Dixon; **p. 9**, Ancient Art and Architecture Collection Ltd/ J Stevens; Bridgeman Art Library **pp. 50** (© Worcester Art Museum, Massachusetts, USA), **20** (Art Gallery and Museum, Kelvingrove, Glasgow, Scotland, © Glasgow City Council (Museums) **23**, (Bibliotheque des Arts Decoratifs, Paris, France, Archives Charmet), **6**, (British Museum, London, UK), **26**, (Galleria degli Uffizi, Florence, Italy, Alinari), **4**, (Louvre, Paris, France), **29**, (Metropolitan Museum of Art, New York, USA), **21**, (Musee Conde, Chantilly, France, Lauros / Giraudon), **28**, (Musee Nat. du Chateau de Malmaison, Rueil-Malmaison, France, Lauros / Giraudon), **34**, (Private Collection), **32** (Private Collection, © Christie's Images), **31**(Private Collection, Index), **47**, (Tretyakov Gallery, Moscow, Russia), **12** (Vatican Museums and Galleries, Vatican City, Italy); Corbis **pp. 43; 13** (Araldo de Luca), **37** (Bettmann), **46** (Bob Roawn; Progressive Image), **39** (Hulton-Deutsch Collection), **14** (Ludovic Maisant); Getty Images **15; 24, 33** (Hulton Archive); **p. 44**, Mary Evans Picture Library; **p. 5**, Neil Burgess Pictures/ Don McCullin; **p. 27**, Rijksmuseum, Amsterdam; **p. 49**, Ronald Grant Archive; **p. 7**, The Ancient Egypt Picture Library; **p. 10**, The Art Archive / National Archaeological Museum Athens / Dagli Orti (A); **p. 35**, The Art Archive/ Imperial War Museum; **p. 36**, The Art Archive/ Imperial War Museum; **p. 17**, Werner Forman Archive/ Biblioteca Universitaria Bologna, Italy. **Cover**: *Shojiro with a sword* by Natori Shunsen, 1924, (colour woodblock print) reproduced with permission of Bridgeman Art Library/ Private Collection.

Contents

Introduction 4

Ancient armies 6

Conquering heroes 10

Dressing for war 14

Native Americans 24

Picturing battles 26

A different view 32

Cartoons, posters, and films 42

War music 46

Stories, plays, and poems 48

Visions of peace 50

Map and Further reading 52

Timeline 53

Glossary 54

Index 56

Any words that appear in bold, **like this**, are explained in the glossary.

Introduction

The stallion rears up on its hind legs, looking terrified. Its rider grasps his sword and stares wildly out of the picture. In the distance, a fire burns out of control.

The painting captures the moment before a violent action. Will the officer use his sword to run through his enemy? Or will he suffer a horrible death? This famous painting shows a scene from the wars of Napoleon Bonaparte in the 19th century. Like many images of conflict, it shows the drama and glamour of battle. However, it also reveals the horror and cruelty of war.

In this book you will see a range of artists' responses to war, dating from **prehistoric** times to the present day. Some portray war as glorious, showing confident armies and triumphant heroes. Others reveal the tragedy of conflict, and the fate of the innocent victims.

Théodore Géricault, *An Officer of the Hussars* (1812). The officer in this painting is dressed as a glamorous hero. But is he brave or terrified? How do you think Géricault feels about war?

4

A range of art

Throughout history, people have been drawn to the subject of war. This book looks at a wide range of art, including paintings, **sculpture**, **tapestries**, and film. It also covers the art of weapon-making and describes the costumes worn in battle.

The book includes masterpieces by famous figures, such as Pablo Picasso, but also shows the work of many lesser-known artists.

Images through the ages

The first five chapters of this book move through different periods of history. Then, later chapters explore how war is shown through other creative arts, such as film, music, and poetry. To help you to see exactly where a work of art was made, there is a map of the world at the end of the book, on page 52. The timeline on page 53 provides an overview of the different periods of history discussed in the book.

The final chapter of this book presents a picture of a world without war. It reveals a vision of a peaceful world where fighting and conflict no longer exist.

In this photograph, taken during the Vietnam War, a young US soldier grasps his gun bravely, while his face expresses horror and fear. As in the Géricault painting, the viewer is left to imagine what the soldier is seeing.

Ancient armies

Around 20,000 years ago, some powerful rulers around the world began to build up armies. The rulers used their armies to protect their kingdoms, and to attack the lands of other rulers. Pictures of armies have been found in ancient palaces and tombs.

The first army?

One of the earliest surviving images of war is found on the Standard of Ur. It was made around 2500 BCE in the land that is now Iraq. The Standard was discovered in a ruler's tomb in one of the world's first cities. Nobody knows exactly what the Standard was used for, but some **archaeologists** believe that it was fixed to a pole and carried like a flag in processions through the city.

The Standard shows a series of scenes from Sumerian life. On one side are images of peace, while on the other side, the Sumerian army is shown marching to war, riding in war chariots, and fighting a battle.

The war-like scenes on the Standard of Ur show the power and force of the Sumerian army. The Sumerian people must have felt that with a powerful army like this, they would be safe. The dramatic scenes also sent out a very clear message to any enemy kingdom – the great Sumerian army should be taken very seriously!

The Standard of Ur is one of the earliest surviving images of war. It shows Sumerian soldiers at war. The figures without uniforms are probably prisoners of war. In the bottom row, fallen enemies are trampled underfoot by the Sumerian horses.

This **fresco** shows Egyptian warriors following their pharaoh into battle. Egyptian warriors went barefoot and wore no armour. They simply relied on their shields to protect them from their enemies' spears.

Armies of Ancient Egypt

About 500 years after the Standard of Ur was made, the Ancient Egyptians began to build up a kingdom on the banks of the River Nile. Powerful **pharaohs** led their armies to war against neighbouring kingdoms. They also kept a permanent army to defend themselves against invaders.

Images of Ancient Egyptian warriors survive in paintings, carvings, and models found in tombs. These images show well-disciplined ranks of foot soldiers, all marching in time with each other.

The foot soldiers are simply dressed in cotton **loincloths**. They carry wooden shields to defend themselves, and they are armed with tall spears. Pharaohs are shown riding to war in light, horse-drawn chariots. They are often shown shooting arrows from large, flexible bows.

The images of Egyptian warriors provide an impressive show of force. They also send out a warning to Egypt's enemies. Anyone who dares to challenge the power of Egypt should fear the mighty pharaoh and his army.

Guardian soldiers

In 221 BCE, Shi Huangdi became the first emperor of China. He was a ruthless leader who was determined to unite the vast Chinese kingdom under his rule. Even after his death, Emperor Shi Huangdi still displayed his power. His tomb was guarded by thousands of life-sized warriors.

Terracotta warriors

The massive burial pit of Emperor Shi Huangdi is filled with an army of over 7,000 warriors. These life-sized figures are made from a type of unglazed pottery called "terracotta". The warriors stand in rows, like a real army. The remains of terracotta horses and bronze chariots and weapons were also found in the pit.

No two terracotta warriors are exactly alike. Each one has a different facial expression or a slightly different uniform, and all the warriors are grouped according to their rank. Many of the figures originally held real weapons – bronze spears, crossbows, and arrows. Some of the crossbows were set to fire automatically at anyone who tried to break into the emperor's tomb.

Yamato guards

The ancient Chinese practice of setting up model soldiers to guard a dead ruler was later copied in Japan. Here, life-sized tomb guardians have been found in the tombs of the Yamato emperors.

They ruled Japan from around 250 to 550 CE. Like the Chinese warriors, the Yamato tomb figures, known as *haniwa*, are made from clay. Some of the models are shown wearing leather armour, like the later **samurai** (see page 22).

Powerful guardians

The model warriors found in Chinese and Japanese tombs provide valuable evidence about the armour and weapons of ancient armies. They also show the power and wealth of the emperors. Some of the warriors served a more practical purpose, too. With their weapons set to fire, they protected the emperor's body from tomb raiders.

Making the warriors

Terracotta is a soft clay that can be easily moulded. The Ancient Chinese potters shaped their figures by hand. Then they used a wooden or metal tool to carve delicate details such as facial features, hair, and armour. Finally, the finished figures were baked slowly over an open fire. When the figures had completely cooled down, they were painted, using a range of natural colours made from powdered rocks and minerals.

Rows of terracotta warriors guard the tomb of China's first emperor. The warriors are incredibly life-like, and they may have been **portraits** of real soldiers.

Conquering heroes

The civilization of Ancient Greece lasted from around 1000 to 150 BCE. The Greeks had a strong and efficient army, which reached its peak under the famous **general**, Alexander the Great. Alexander led the Greek army in a series of conquests, winning land in the Middle East and India. Many people consider him to be the greatest general who has ever lived.

Images of Alexander

For the Ancient Greeks, Alexander was a super-hero. Greek historians and poets told the story of his adventures, while the work of painters, **sculptors**, and **mosaic** makers made him instantly recognized all over the Greek world.

One of the earliest **portraits** of Alexander appeared on coins that were issued during his reign (time as leader). The coins show him wearing a helmet made from a lion's head. The face of the young hero stares out bravely from inside the lion's jaws. It gives a striking impression of daring and strength.

Alexander was also shown in action. A large mosaic discovered in southern Italy shows the Greeks' victory over the Persians at the battle of Issus. In the centre of the mosaic, Alexander is shown on a horse, charging bravely towards the enemy. Meanwhile, King Darius of Persia has turned his chariot.

He flees in terror from the battlefield. The mosaic gives a powerful sense of the drama and confusion of war. It also contrasts Alexander's bravery with the cowardly behaviour of the Persian commander.

A stone head of Alexander, wearing his war headdress made from a lion's head. Even though this statue is damaged, it is still clear that Alexander is presented as a young and handsome hero.

Heroes of war

Alexander was not the only Greek war hero. Hector, Achilles, and Odysseus were also great military leaders who had poems and plays written about them.

The most famous Greek war poem was the *Iliad*, which was written by Homer. The *Iliad* tells the adventures of Odysseus in the Greek wars against the Trojans, and his plan to capture the city of Troy.

He sent a huge wooden horse as a gift to the people of Troy. This "gift" was secretly filled with Greek soldiers.

Warriors on vases

Many Ancient Greek vases feature paintings of warriors in action. The warriors wear short tunics and elegant plumed helmets. They hold circular shields and fight with long spears.

The "Alexander mosaic" discovered at Pompeii, showing Alexander's victory at the Battle of Issus in 33 BCE. Alexander is on the left of the mosaic, preparing to throw his spear. On the right-hand side of the picture, the cowardly King Darius flees from the battlefield in his chariot.

Roman heroes

By the first century BCE, the Greeks were losing power. In their place, the Romans became the most powerful people in the area around the Mediterranean Sea. Then the Romans started to conquer new land. Gradually, they built up a vast empire.

A series of brilliant army generals led the **campaigns** to win land for the Empire. These outstanding military leaders were often emperors as well. They were remembered and honoured with grand statues and monuments.

Statues and monuments

The Emperor Augustus was an excellent general who won large areas of land for Rome. In order to recognize his achievements, a larger-than-life statue of Augustus was carved out of marble. This striking work of art shows Augustus dressed in his general's uniform, with one hand raised to command his troops. The statue gives an overwhelming impression of the power and strength of the Roman leader.

A marble statue of the Emperor Augustus, made around 20 BCE to celebrate one of his greatest military victories. The carvings on his battle tunic show the leader of the defeated army surrendering.

As well as carving statues, the Romans also built massive monuments to remind the people of their triumphs in war. One of the first military monuments was built by the Emperor Trajan. After his victories in Eastern Europe, Trajan had a tall column erected in Rome, with a golden statue of himself on its top. Trajan's column is covered with a series of scenes showing the Roman army in action. The column is 30 metres (100 feet) high. It could be seen for miles around and it provided a lasting record of the Romans' success.

Another famous monument was built to celebrate the victory of the Emperor Constantine over his rival, Maxentius, in 312 CE. This monument took the form of an enormous marble arch, which was covered with carvings.

The carvings show Constantine's battles. Constantine's arch was the last of a series of arches built in Rome. These impressive arches were used as the focus for processions through the city. In these grand processions, military heroes drove their chariots in triumph through the archway.

Columns and arches

The Roman practice of building victory columns and arches was copied by later civilizations. Nelson's column in London commemorates the victory of the British navy over Napoleon's French army at the Battle of Trafalgar in 1805. The Arc de Triomphe in Paris was built to celebrate Napoleon's victories in the early 1800s.

This detail from Trajan's column shows the Roman army fighting against the Dacians (a fierce German tribe). The Romans wear armour, carry large shields, and fight with swords. However, the Dacians wear basic trousers and fight with wooden clubs. What message do you think the sculptor was trying to give about the Romans and their enemies?

Dressing for war

In many **indigenous** cultures, warriors wear very distinctive clothing. They may wear a special mask or headdress, or they may decorate their bodies with colours and patterns that have a special meaning. Wearing a traditional costume can connect a warrior with his **ancestors** and with past battles of his people. Costumes may also be associated with a particular god or spirit. So, if someone wears a mask **depicting** a spirit, they take on some of the powers of that spirit. Special battle dress also has the effect of making warriors look very frightening.

African traditions

In many parts of Africa, warrior traditions still survive. Craft workers still carve warrior masks and make shields and headdresses, and people still perform ancient war ceremonies and dances.

Each different tribal group has its own traditions, costumes, and weapons. However, these weapons and costumes are no longer used for battle. When Africans get involved in wars today, they fight with modern weapons.

Grebo masks

The Grebo people of West Africa carve war masks with small, round eyes to represent alertness and anger. Grebo masks also have a sharp, straight nose, rather like a bird's beak. The sharp nose shows that the mask's wearer is fierce and determined, and unwilling to retreat in battle. A carved block under the nose represents teeth, and the teeth are bared to show **aggression**. Today, Grebo masks are worn for traditional dances and ceremonies.

The patterns and colours on these shields have special meanings for the Masai people. In traditional African warfare, warriors believed that symbols like these helped to protect them.

Masai warriors

Masai warriors from East Africa often decorate their bodies and faces for their ceremonial war dances. They use a white **pigment** to paint dramatic stripes and **geometric** patterns on their skin. The warriors also carry painted shields and wear headdresses made from animals' skin and feathers. This special "battle dress" makes the warriors appear very frightening.

Maori tattoos

For many centuries, **Maori** warriors in New Zealand had traditional patterns **tattooed** onto their faces. These striking designs made them look especially fierce in battle. The tattoos were created by making a series of deep cuts in the skin, using a sharp chisel made from bone. These cuts were filled with natural pigments made from powdered rocks. Tattooing was a long and painful process and there was always a danger of infection. A warrior's tattoos were a sign of his bravery and physical endurance.

A Maori dressed in traditional costume performing *haka* – a wild dance of warriors before battle. This man also has traditional patterns tattooed on his face, making him look very fierce.

Performing haka

In the past, Maori warriors performed a wild dance, known as *haka*, before they charged into battle. *Haka* involves fierce shouting, flexing the arms, and stamping the feet. Today, the New Zealand All Blacks rugby team perform *haka* before they start to play a match.

Maya and Aztec knights

Around 300 BCE, a war-like people called the Maya began to build stone cities deep in the rainforests of Central America. A thousand years later, the **Aztec** people settled in the same area. Both these cultures flourished until the 16th century, when Spanish conquerors arrived in America.

Feathers and skins

Warfare played a central part in the life of the Maya and the Aztecs. It was a great honour to be a warrior, and their proud warrior **knights** wore distinctive clothing made by skilled craft workers.

Maya knights wore stunning costumes made from spotted jaguar skins and the colourful feathers of rainforest birds. Maya headdresses, tunics, wristbands, and boots were all made from feathers and animal skins. The towering headdresses of the Maya knights often featured the heads of fierce beasts and birds.

The fiercest and bravest warriors in the Aztec army were the eagle and jaguar knights. Aztec eagle knights wore a costume made almost entirely from golden eagle feathers. A pair of eagle claws covered the eagle knight's feet. A long, feathered tail was attached to the back of his tunic, and his headdress was shaped like an eagle's beak. Jaguar knights wore tunics made from spotted jaguar skins and a headdress constructed from a jaguar's head.

Special powers

When Aztec knights dressed as eagles or jaguars, they believed that they became as fearless as these creatures. Warriors believed that costumes made from the skin and feathers of fierce beasts gave their wearers special powers. In particular, the vivid green feathers of the **sacred** Quetzal bird, worn by the Maya and the Aztecs, were believed to protect warriors in battle.

Carvings and codices

We have plenty of evidence of how the Mayan and Aztec warriors looked, thanks to their skilful carvers and artists.

The Maya people built stone **pyramids** for their gods, and covered them with carvings. Some of these carvings still survive today. They show warriors and their leaders fighting wars and taking part in ceremonies. Mayan artists also produced **codices**, an early type of folded book, which told the history of their people. These colourful picture books contain many portraits of warriors dressed in elaborate costumes.

The Aztecs also built pyramids, but they have not survived. However, Aztec codices illustrate the history of the Aztecs and their battles. They include some dramatic portraits of eagle and jaguar knights.

This picture from an Aztec codex shows two knights, dressed in full battle gear, with elaborate headdresses. The warrior on the right is a jaguar knight.

Medieval soldiers

Around the year 1000 CE, a new kind of warrior emerged in Europe. Powerful lords began to use bands of trained soldiers to defend their castles and to launch attacks on rival lords. These early **medieval** soldiers dressed for battle in **chain-mail** tunics made from linked metal rings. They wore metal helmets and carried long, wooden shields to protect themselves.

Most of the early medieval soldiers fought on foot, using long spears or bows and arrows, but some fought on horseback with spears and swords. Warhorses were very expensive, so mounted soldiers had to be wealthy men. These skilled, mounted warriors were the first medieval knights.

Books about knights

By the 13th century, many hand-written books, known as **manuscripts**, had been produced on the subject of knights. Histories of war recorded brave deeds performed by knights. Guides for knights explained how a perfect knight should behave. There were also many poems, stories, and songs about the adventures of brave young knights. These medieval manuscripts were often beautifully illustrated or "**illuminated**". Manuscript illuminations show knights in armour, fighting battles and setting off on adventures. In these works, the knights are usually shown as courageous heroes.

The Bayeux Tapestry

The best surviving images of early medieval warfare are found in the Bayeux Tapestry, which was made around 1070. The tapestry tells the story of the Norman Conquest in 1066, when an army of Normans from northern France attacked and conquered England. It works rather like a modern comic strip, with a sequence of action-packed scenes, accompanied by a few words of text.

The Bayeux Tapestry was made for William the Conqueror to celebrate his victory, and to provide a record of his successful military campaign. It supplies valuable evidence on the way that soldiers were dressed, and the way that battles were fought in the 11th century. It also shows how the Normans prepared for battle and transported their troops across the English Channel.

The Knights of the Round Table

Perhaps the most famous of all the stories of knights were the legends of King Arthur and his companions. In the 12th and 13th centuries, these legends were sung and told to young knights. Later they were written down in manuscripts. In these fantastic tales, figures such as Sir Lancelot and Sir Gawain experience a series of "trials", all designed to test their bravery, loyalty, and truthfulness. The stories provided a shining example of how the perfect knight should behave.

MAR E

The Bayeux Tapestry provides a detailed record of the Norman Conquest of England in 1066. In this scene, Norman knights and their horses are crossing the English Channel, ready to launch their attack on the Anglo-Saxons. The soldiers' large shields are hung on the back of the boats.

Medieval arms and armour

Later medieval knights wore elaborate suits of armour made from shaped and decorated metal plates. The plates were fitted with joints and hinges to allow the knight to move. These plate-armour suits covered most of the knight's body and were usually made to measure. Only very specialized metal workers could produce suits of armour. The best suits were made by families working in Germany and northern Italy.

Making weapons and shields was a highly skilled art. Some medieval swords and daggers were decorated with inlaid patterns made from other metals. These splendid weapons were often used for ceremonies rather than real battles. Metal workers also constructed more unusual weapons, such as the morning star – a ball covered with spikes on the end of a chain with a handle.

Playing at war

In the 15th and 16th centuries, many kings and lords held elaborate **tournaments**. These exciting events gave knights the chance to practise their battle skills by competing against each other. The main attraction of the tournament was the **joust** – a formal mock battle.

Suit of armour made in Germany for the Emperor Maximilian around 1510. By the 16th century, suits of armour had become incredibly elaborate. They were made by skilled metal workers and were works of art in their own right.

Jousts were held on a special ground, known as a tilting yard. The tilting yard had two long tracks, separated by a low wooden bar. In a joust, two knights on horseback charged towards each other. Each knight carried a lance or long pole, with which he tried to knock his opponent to the ground. Jousts were very popular with ladies, who often gave a sign of their **favour**, such as a scarf, to their favourite knight.

Tournaments were often shown in paintings and described in poems, songs and stories. Some medieval legends include a dramatic joust, in which a mysterious knight challenges the other knights to fight.

The art of heraldry

Once a medieval knight was dressed in full armour, he was very hard to recognize, so a system gradually developed to make knights easy to identify in battle. Knights carried shields painted with their personal **coat of arms**. They also often wore a coat of arms on their chest and carried a tall banner, which could be spotted from a long way off.

Very soon, however, coats of arms became too complicated for most people to remember. This meant that experts, called heralds-at-arms, had to be employed on the battlefield and in tournaments. The herald recognized a knight's coat of arms and called out who he was. So, "heraldry" is the recognition and design of coats of arms. It is still practised today.

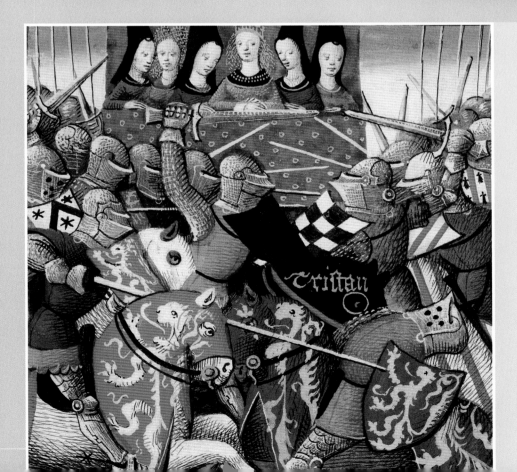

Medieval artists painted colourful pictures of tournaments. Here, a queen and her ladies-in- waiting watch very calmly as two groups of knights fight a mock battle.

21

Arab warriors

In the 8th century CE **Arab** warriors began to conquer land in the Middle East. They rode on swift horses and fought with axes and curved swords known as "scimitars". The Arabs established a large **Islamic** Empire, which covered the Middle East, southern Spain, and North Africa. They also conquered land in India.

Arab weapons

The tradition of making scimitars, axes, swords, and shields flourished all over the Islamic world. Some of the finest examples of weapons are found in northern India, where metal workers created elaborate daggers, axes, and swords inlaid with enamel. These weapons were works of art in their own right and were often used purely for ceremonies.

Japanese samurai

While knights were fighting battles and living in castles in Europe, a class of war-like, castle-dwelling warriors was also emerging in Japan. Around 1200 CE, powerful warlords, called "shoguns", took over the running of Japan. The shoguns relied on warriors called "**samurai**" to fight for them and to drive away invaders.

The samurai lived in castles and trained for battle. They defended their castle against enemies and launched savage attacks on neighbouring castles. The samurai continued their war-like ways until the 19th century.

The common use of gunpowder at that time brought an end to the Samurai tradition.

Samurai costumes and weapons

Samurai warriors wore armour made from strips of leather. These leather strips were usually stitched together with silk and protected by a layer of lacquer (varnish). Samurai wore straw sandals and elaborate horned headdresses. Some warriors also wore carved and painted masks to appear more frightening.

The early samurai fought with bows and arrows, batons, and swords, but their long curved sword, or *katana*, was their most important weapon. The tradition of fighting with swords continued right up to the 19th century, although some samurai also used **muskets**. Samurai swords and muskets were exquisitely decorated, with inlays of precious metal and mother-of-pearl.

Samurai paintings

In the 19th century, some Japanese artists produced vivid **watercolours** of fighting Samurai. These stylized paintings show warriors with fierce, grimacing expressions fighting a duel with swords. The warriors wear richly patterned robes and are shown in athletic but graceful poses. Many of the paintings show the Samurai battles taking place against a background of dramatic scenery. The painted battles appear to be slightly dream-like and unreal – more like a **formal** dance than a serious battle.

芳年武者无類

左兵衛佐源頼朝

This 19th-century Japanese print shows two samurai fighting. The colourful patterns on the samurai's costumes seem to be just as important as the action to the artist.

The art of duelling

It was not just the Japanese samurai who practiced organized fighting with swords or pistols. In Europe, from the **Middle Ages** until the 19th century, a quarrel between two gentlemen was often settled by a duel. Duels were fought with swords until the 1600s, and later with pistols, and they followed very strict rules.

Many writers have included dramatic duels in their plays and novels. In William Shakespeare's play *Romeo and Juliet*, Romeo becomes involved in a duel in which his best friend is killed. The French artist Jean-Léon Gérôme also showed the tragic result of a duel in his painting *Duel after a Masked Ball* (1857). In this painting, a man dressed as a clown is shown dying from his wounds.

Native Americans

Around 15,000 years ago, people started arriving in the northernmost areas of the vast continent of North America. They had walked across a bridge of ice from Siberia, now in northern Russia. Very gradually, these people travelled southwards and spread out, until there were tribes living in most areas of North America. Each tribe adopted a different way of life, depending on where they had settled, and every tribe had its own traditions and types of dress. Many of these traditions were associated with war.

Dressed for battle

The warriors of the central plains have been pictured in many paintings and photographs. They wore tunics made from buffalo skin, decorated with **porcupine quillwork** running up the sleeves and across the shoulders. Their fringed leggings were also made from soft leather, and on their feet were leather moccasins, decorated with beads and quills. The warriors' long hair was carefully brushed and greased. Some of them wore an elaborate feathered headdress, known as a "war bonnet". Each part of a warrior's costume had a special significance, which could be recognized by other Native Americans.

The language of feathers

The war bonnets of the Plains Indians were made from the feathers of wild birds, such as eagles and turkeys. Each feather in the bonnet tells a story about the bonnet's wearer. For example, an upright feather with a strip of horsehair attached to it shows that the wearer has won a victory in a hand-to-hand fight; a red feather indicates that he has been wounded; and a feather with a red dot means that the wearer has killed an enemy.

A portrait of a Sioux chief, wearing a war bonnet. The chief is holding a pipe of peace.

Counting coup

The leggings worn by the Plains Indian were marked by horizontal "coup (*coo*) marks". In Native American culture, "coup" was the act of touching an enemy in the heat of battle with a coup stick or with the flat of a hand. The number of coup marks worn by a warrior showed his courage in battle.

George Catlin (1796–1872)

The American painter George Catlin originally trained as a lawyer, but at the age of 28 he decided to devote his life to painting Native Americans and studying their traditions. Working mainly in Nebraska and Missouri, he painted portraits of individual chiefs and **braves** and also showed battles and ceremonies. Catlin wrote a series of letters describing the customs of Native American tribes. In some of these letters he describes the practice of counting coup marks.

George Catlin, *Battle between Sioux and Fox* (1846–1848). Catlin was fascinated by the Native Americans, and tried to show their way of life as accurately as he could.

Picturing battles

By the 15th century, some wealthy people in Europe were paying artists to paint battle scenes. These powerful figures wanted to have a picture in their home that showed their side winning a glorious victory. Many talented artists rose to this challenge. They painted dramatic scenes that made war look exciting and glamorous.

Uccello's battles

It was fashionable in the 15th century to show personal battle victories in paintings. To make the victory look more impressive, artists often exaggerated. Paolo Uccello created three huge paintings of scenes from the Battle of San Romano. Far from being a scene of mass slaughter, as shown in this huge picture, the actual fight was very small. Art is used here to make the winner, Niccolò Mauruzi da Tolentino, seem more important. The paintings are full of action, as mounted knights charge at each other with long spears. Uccello's picture-book image of war is partly true. In 15th-century Italy, most battles took place at agreed times and did not involve massive slaughter. Although ordinary soldiers were killed, their commanders were usually unharmed. The main aim of a battle was to capture wealthy knights, and demand a **ransom** for their release.

Paolo Uccello, Part of *The Battle of San Romano* (c.1450). Uccello's battle scene shows mounted knights fighting with long wooden lances, and foot soldiers firing crossbows. Even though some soldiers and horses have fallen, there is still a sense that the battle is simply a colourful game.

Cornelis Claesz van Wieringen, *The Explosion of the Spanish Flagship during the Battle of Gibraltar* (c.1621). This dramatic scene gives a powerful sense of the chaos and destruction of a battle at sea. However, the figures are too small to see the responses of individual sailors.

Battles at sea

By the 1550s, more and more battles were being fought at sea. This resulted in a new type of painting showing **maritime** battles. The leading maritime artists of the 16th and 17th centuries came from the Netherlands. They recorded the triumphs of the Dutch navy in paintings that showed the big picture, rather than the details of a battle. This "big picture" viewpoint was also used for showing battles on land.

One of the best-known Dutch maritime artists was Cornelis Claesz van Wieringen (c.1580–1633). His large-scale oil paintings show dramatic sea battles between the Spanish and Dutch navies. In these highly detailed works, graceful-looking battleships engage in battle under threatening skies filled with **cannon** smoke. The total effect is like a grand show. Although the artist shows some figures, they are much too small to give a sense of the sailors' experience of war.

A romantic view

Around 1800, some artists in Europe began to paint more glamorous images of war and conflict. These artists belonged to the **Romantic** Movement, which continued until the 1850s. The Romantics tried to describe how it might feel to be in a certain situation. They did this with dramatic poses and colours. Their paintings of war were not intended to be realistic, as they were more interested in showing emotion.

Napoleon the hero

One of the leading members of the Romantic Movement was the French artist Jacques-Louis David. In 1801, David painted a dramatic portrait called *Napoleon Crossing the Alps*. This famous painting shows the French general as a dashing hero, dressed in a swirling scarlet cloak.

While his terrified horse rears up in dismay at the prospect of the steep mountain path ahead, Napoleon is completely undaunted. He gazes calmly out of the picture, one arm raised and pointing at the distant horizon where he and his troops are heading. Meanwhile, the ghostly figures of soldiers can be glimpsed behind their leader, dragging huge cannon up the mountainside. The painting presents an image of war as a glorious triumph over difficulties, and celebrates the idea of a warrior leader.

An inspiring moment

In about 1835, another leading French Romantic artist, Eugéne Delacroix, painted *The Battle of Taillebourg*. The painting shows King Louis IX of France on his white horse, charging through the enemy English army. This daring act was the start of Louis' successful attempts to claim French land back from the English in the **Middle Ages**.

Jacques-Louis David, *Napoleon Crossing the Alps* (1801). David's famous portrait shows Napoleon as a fearless leader. But this is not the painting's only message. Look at the tiny figures, trudging up the hill behind him.

Delacroix's painting was intended to give the French pride and passion for their country. His goal was not simply to show the event, although the details are carefully researched and the armour and banners are historically correct. Through his exciting painting, with its hero at its centre, Delacroix wanted to make the viewer feel the emotion of the moment.

An American hero

Emanuel Gottlieb Leutze worked in America and Germany, and painted historical themes in a Romantic style.

Leutze's most famous work, *Washington Crossing the Delaware* (1851), shows an inspiring, dramatic scene from the American Revolutionary War. Washington is portrayed as a heroic leader encouraging his loyal troops to cross the frozen river early on Christmas morning. In fact, the reality was very different. Washington's troops were poorly armed and desperate with cold and hunger, and were on the point of deserting their leader.

Emanuel Gottlieb Leutze, *Washington Crossing the Delaware* (1851). In this famous painting, Leutze presents a romantic view of Washington's river crossing. The real event was very different.

Goya's nightmare vision

While the Romantic painters were presenting their glamourized images of war, other artists were showing how the victims of war suffered. The Spanish artist Francisco de Goya lived from 1746 to 1828 and witnessed the horrors of Napoleon's invasion of Spain. He was appalled by what he saw.

In 1814, Goya painted his famous work *The Executions of the Third of May, 1808*. It shows a shooting party of French soldiers executing a group of Spanish rebels at night. While the soldiers with their guns are shadowy, almost mechanical figures, the next man facing the firing squad is brilliantly lit by a lantern. His desperate friends and supporters are grouped around him. Meanwhile the previous victims of the shooting party lie soaked with blood in the foreground of the painting.

Altogether, Goya's painting sends out an unmistakable message that war is cruel and inhuman. It was the first time that the realities of war had been depicted in such a stark and effective way.

Francisco de Goya, *The Executions of the Third of May, 1808* (1814). The terrified but defiant expression on the victim's face is the most important part of Goya's powerful painting. In contrast, the executioners are inhuman, almost mechanical figures.

Disasters of War

Between the years 1810 and 1820, Goya produced a series of 82 **prints** known as *Disasters of War*. In these shocking images, Goya focuses on what happens to individuals in war. His prints include close-up images of violent stabbings and other brutal acts, and feature horrific portraits of pain and suffering. They are among the most powerful images of war that were ever created.

Goya produced his *Disasters of War* as a private project, and the prints were never published during his lifetime. However, they later became very famous. The *Disasters* had a powerful influence on the war images of later artists, such as Käthe Kollwitz and Pablo Picasso (see pages 38–39 and 40–41).

Goya's message

Goya based his images of war on real scenes that he had seen during the French invasion of Spain. But in spite of all the cruelty he saw, Goya's works were not intended as a direct attack on the French army. Instead, Goya's aim was to show the pity and horror of war. In his paintings and prints, the soldiers and their victims seem to be timeless. They could come from any time or place. Goya shows the universal tragedy of war.

A modern view

In 1993, British artists Jake and Dinos Chapman created a work called *Disasters of War* as a tribute to Goya and a commentary on the horror of war. Their work is a collection of intricately painted miniature battle scenes, laid out in a transparent plastic case like a collection of model soldiers. The Chapman brothers' work comments on people's fascination with war, which still continues today, almost 200 years after Goya's powerful protest.

Francisco de Goya, *They do not know the way*, plate 70 of *Disasters of War*. Goya's shadowy prisoners, stumbling blindly through a rocky landscape, seem like figures in a nightmare.

A different view

By the second half of the 19th century, many artists were depicting war in a more realistic way. This changing approach can be seen in art from the **American Civil War**, which lasted from 1861 to 1865. Some artists painted what daily life was like for the soldiers. They showed the hard work and dirt, as well as the danger and friendship. These images helped people at home understand the soldiers' lives better.

Winslow Homer

During the American Civil War, people followed the news of the conflict with great interest. The young artist Winslow Homer worked for the popular magazine *Harper's Weekly*. Homer produced vivid, realistic images of battle. However, he preferred to concentrate on individual soldiers. He produced some striking portraits of men in action, such as *Yankee Sharpshooter*, which shows a young rifleman perched in a tree. He also painted portraits of soldiers off duty. For example, in his painting *Home Sweet Home*, Homer shows a couple of soldiers relaxing by their tents. Images like this gave the American public a sense of what everyday life was like for the ordinary soldiers.

Winslow Homer, *Home Sweet Home* (1863). Homer was one of the first artists to show soldiers off duty. This painting became very popular.

One of Mathew Brady's shocking photographs, taken on the battlefields of the American Civil War. Nobody had ever seen war images like this, and the American people were horrified.

Captain James Hope

A different vision of war was produced by Captain James Hope. He joined the **Union army** as a regular soldier, but after he was wounded stayed on as an artist. Hope saw the conflict through the eyes of a soldier, and tried to give an accurate impression of battle, especially when things went wrong. His paintings of the American Civil War have names like *Artillery Hell*, *A Fateful Turn*, and *Wasted Gallantry*.

Mathew Brady

One of the artists who made the most difference to the way the public saw the war was Mathew Brady. Brady was one of the earliest war photographers. In 1861, he abandoned his career as a portrait photographer and headed for the battlefront. There, he organized a band of photographers to follow the troops into battle and record the action.

In 1862, Brady shocked the American public by displaying his photos of **corpses** on the battlefield at Antietam. This exhibition was the first time most people had witnessed the **carnage** of war. An article in the *New York Times* reported that Brady had brought "home to us the terrible reality and earnestness of war".

Recording World War I

By the time World War I began in 1914, the profession of the war artist was well established. Artists went to war with the troops and lived alongside them. They suffered the same dangers as the soldiers, and were sometimes wounded or even killed.

During World War I, artists showed life in the trenches and on the battlefield. Photographers also recorded the war, but photographic equipment was hard to transport, so artists with their sketchpads had a very important role to play.

Artists of World War I

One of the most respected artists of World War I was the Australian George Lambert. He accompanied troops to Gallipoli, in the Middle East, and produced over 500 sketches and paintings. Lambert also introduced a new type of military portrait. Instead of showing his subjects as dashing heroes, he concentrated on their real characters. Lambert's portraits of Australian officers and sergeants showed simple farmers far from home.

The British artist Christopher Nevinson spent several months at the Western front, where fighting was happening on the borders of France and Belgium. Nevinson sketched soldiers in action and was fascinated by the new machinery of war.

Several of his paintings show men using enormous machine guns. In these stark images, the machines seem to take over.

Another British artist with a very personal vision was Stanley Spencer. He helped in a soldiers' hospital in Eastern Europe during the war. After the conflict was over, Spencer created a series of large-scale canvases for the Burghclere Chapel in Hampshire, England. Spencer's paintings concentrate on the sick and the dying and the people who cared for them. They show medical workers carrying the wounded on stretchers, and working in crowded hospital wards.

Christopher Nevinson, *La Mitrailleuse (The Machine Gun)* (1915). The machine gun is the focus, but there are also four figures. Why do you think that Nevinson chose to show war like this?

John Singer Sargent, *Gassed* (1919). Sargent's haunting painting of the blinded victims of mustard gas is an unforgettable image of the terrible suffering caused by war.

Gassed

At the end of World War I, the famous American painter John Singer Sargent was **commissioned** by the Imperial War Museum in London to create a centrepiece for their Hall of Remembrance. Sargent decided that he would show a group of soldiers suffering from the terrible effects of "mustard gas", which was used in some battles.

Sargent spent four months in a French hospital for wounded soldiers, making studies for his painting. *Gassed* shows a line of choking and blinded soldiers, clutching onto each other and stumbling across a field. It presents an unforgettable image of the pain and horror of war.

Artists of World War II

World War II posed many challenges for artists. It was fought on many different fronts all over the world. It also involved huge amounts of equipment and machinery. Photographers recorded all aspects of the conflict, but artists still had an important role to play.

The British landscape painter Paul Nash concentrated on the war in the air. His painting *Battle of Germany* presents an almost **abstract** image of flying planes and bombs. Nash's most famous image of war, *The Dead Sea*, shows a sea of crashed planes in a barren landscape. The wreckage of the planes forms a pattern of broken shapes that gives the viewer an uncomfortable sense of harshness and destruction.

The sculptor and artist Henry Moore made a series of drawings of Londoners sleeping in the train tunnels of the Underground to stay safe from the bombs. In Moore's haunting drawings, the sleeping figures seem hardly human. Instead, their bundled shapes look like large and ghostly butterfly cocoons. The viewer is given the sense that the war has created a new kind of weird, underground world.

Paul Nash, *The Battle of Germany* (1944). In his painting of a battle in the air, Nash has created a frightening landscape filled with billowing smoke and flames.

Photographs of World War II

The events of World War II were recorded in black and white photographs and on cinematic film (see page 45). Striking photographs appeared in weekly magazines like *Picture Post*. These images showed troops fighting on the ground, at sea, and in the air. They also showed how the war affected the lives of the people who stayed at home.

Some outstanding photos had a powerful effect on the public and were reproduced many times. One dramatic image shows a view of the city of London after a heavy bombing raid. Most of the buildings are hidden in smoke and dust, but rising above the dust is the untouched dome of St Paul's Cathedral. This picture was a symbol of hope and endurance for British people during the war.

Some **ciné** films showed the D-Day landings on the shores of northern France. These films give a vivid impression of the chaos and confusion of war. At the end of the war, some tragic but unforgettable images were published in the press. The shocking portraits of concentration camp survivors brought a new horror to the eyes of the world.

One of the most famous photographs of World War II shows the spreading mushroom cloud of the atomic bomb which was dropped on the Japanese

The atom bomb explodes in a mushroom-shaped cloud over the city of Hiroshima. This photograph is one of the world's most famous images of war.

city of Hiroshima. This simple image became a famous symbol of the deadly power of war. In one dramatic image, it revealed our newly found ability to cause death and destruction on a scale never before imagined.

Images of pain

During the 20th century, artists began to concentrate on the victims of war. In particular, they presented the sufferings of innocent women and children who had been caught up in terrible conflicts all over the world.

A mother's pain

One artist who showed this pain was Käthe Kollwitz, who lived in Germany in the early 20th century. Soon after the start of World War I, her son joined the German army. He was killed in action in 1914. This personal tragedy, and her observations of the sufferings of others, prompted her to produce a series of **prints** on the subject of war. These works showed the impact of war on **civilians**, and especially on women and their children.

Käthe Kollwitz worked mainly in black and white, but sometimes used touches of colour to highlight her subjects. Many of her works show mothers mourning for their sons or grieving widows protecting their children. One distressing drawing, simply called *Battlefield*, shows a woman checking bodies on a battlefield to find her man. Another, called *The Mothers*, pictures a group of desperate women all huddled together for comfort.

Käthe Kollwitz, *The Mothers* (1921) Number six from *Seven Woodcuts of War*. In this powerful image, the mothers form a rock-like shape, protecting their children from attack. At first, you only notice the mothers, but then you begin to see their children too.

One of Kollwitz's most memorable images shows a desperate but defiant woman, raising one arm above her head as if to stop the advancing troops. It is entitled *War – Never Again!*.

Photographing pain

Ever since Mathew Brady photographed the battlefields of the American Civil War, photographers have played an important part in recording war and conflict. During the first half of the 20th century, dramatic black-and-white photographs appeared in weekly magazines, accompanied by short captions. This form of visual reporting, known as "photojournalism", often featured images of war. The art of photojournalism lasted into the 1980s, but has now been replaced by TV reports and documentaries.

However, photographs of war are still published in newspapers around the world.

In order to give an impression of the terrible impact of a war, photographers often concentrate on just a few victims. A dramatic moment was captured by the Hungarian photographer Robert Capa during the Spanish Civil War (see page 40). Capa's striking photograph shows a Spanish soldier seconds after he was shot, falling gracefully to his death. One of the most famous war photographs was taken by the Vietnamese photographer Nic Ut. This image from the Vietnam War was taken in 1972. It shows a group of desperate children running down a road to escape from a **napalm** attack in their village.

An action shot taken during the Vietnam War. By the 1960s, cameras were light and easy to carry. This meant war photographers could record events as they happened.

Picasso's *Guernica*

Perhaps the most powerful protest against war during the 20th century was made by the Spanish artist Pablo Picasso. His **mural**, *Guernica*, has been described as the world's most famous anti-war statement.

Early in 1937, Picasso was asked to paint a giant mural. This mural was to be the centrepiece for the Spanish Pavilion in the World Fair, to be held in Paris. Picasso wanted his work to represent the spirit of the Spanish people, but he was uncertain what subject to show. Then, in April 1937, some tragic events in a small Spanish village made it obvious to him what subject he should choose.

The massacre at Guernica

From 1936 to 1937, Spain was divided by a bitter **civil war**. One side was led by General Franco, who was supported by Hitler's **Nazi party**. On the other side, the **Republicans** were fighting to keep their country free. In April 1937, Franco gave permission for Hitler's planes to practise their new bombing techniques. The target he selected was the village of Guernica, in northern Spain. Hitler's planes bombarded the village for three hours, flattening buildings, and killing or wounding 1,600 people.

News of the **massacre** soon reached Paris, where Picasso was working. Stunned by the photographs and reports from Spain, he started work on his mural immediately.

Picasso's famous mural expresses the pain of the people of Guernica, a small Spanish village that was flattened by bombs. It is a powerful protest against the cruelty of war. The painting is filled with fragments of people, and animals in pain. Why do you think Picasso chose to paint his mural in such a broken-up style?

A shocking vision

Picasso decided not to represent the horror of Guernica in a realistic way. Instead he showed just the bare elements of figures and animals. Some of the subjects in his mural are a screaming mother holding her child, a man with outstretched arms, a bull, and an agonized horse. Picasso combined these elements into one composition, full of fragments and jagged shapes.

In *Guernica*, pale figures and animals are set against a dark and sombre background, as if a spotlight is being shone on their agony. Faces and arms seem to reach out from the shadows.

Some figures are running, while others are lying dead on the ground. Altogether, the mural gives a vivid impression of the horror and inhumanity of war.

Cubism

Picasso's *Guernica* is painted in the Cubist style. This style was developed by Picasso and a French artist, Georges Braque, in the early 20th century. They made all human and natural forms into simple **geometric** shapes. They also tried to make flat painting three-dimensional by showing different sides of a form. This gives the figures and objects a disjointed appearance, and adds to the chaotic feeling of *Guernica*.

41

Cartoons, posters, and films

In times of conflict and danger, governments need to communicate with the people of their country. One very effective way to do this is through posters. Over the last hundred years, governments at war have frequently commissioned artists and designers to create eye-catching posters.

Powerful posters

Wartime posters can have many uses. Often they are used to recruit people to fight for a cause. In 1914, following the outbreak of World War I, the British government came up with the idea of showing Lord Kitchener, the head of the army, dressed in full uniform and pointing straight out of the poster. The message underneath this imposing figure read, "Your country needs you." Three years later in 1917, the American designer James Montgomery Flagg adapted this idea, showing a giant "Uncle Sam" with the slogan, "I want you for the U.S. army."

Posters for the home front

Posters produced in wartime are also used to encourage people based at home. During World War II, the British and US governments both produced posters reminding workers who stayed at home that they were also helping to win the war. These posters were aimed especially at women, who had taken over the jobs of the absent soldiers.

One famous US poster featured a tough female character nicknamed "Rosie the riveter". The poster had the slogan, "We Can Do It!"

During the two World Wars, several governments ran poster campaigns warning the public against "careless talk". These posters sent out the message that talking about where the troops were heading next could be very dangerous if this news was overheard by enemy spies. One American poster from World War II features a dramatic image of a sinking ship behind the boldly printed message "Loose Lips might Sink Ships".

War cartoons

Cartoons showing people at war have a very long history. As early as the 1850s, artists were producing cartoons of war to be published in magazines. These images often took the form of savage attacks on cruel and stupid war leaders. For example, an ink drawing produced by Joseph Paton in 1855 shows the commander of the British army in the Crimean War as the figure of Death riding through a battlefield of **corpses**.

This American poster from World War II shows Rosie the Riveter, a female worker in a factory producing war equipment. Rosie is telling all her fellow women that they can help to win the war.

Soldiers in cartoons

Some of the greatest war cartoonists have shown the experience of soldiers and tried to represent their point of view.

During World War I, British cartoonist Bruce Bairnsfather created the character of Old Bill, based partly on his own experiences in the trenches.

Bruce Bairnsfather's cartoons featured Old Bill, a World War I soldier who refuses to panic, even when his life is in danger. Here, Old Bill gives another soldier a haircut, completely ignoring the bombs that fly overhead.

Old Bill represents the patient soldier, who is never scared by anything, even when the enemy fires directly at him.

Soldiers from all over the world identified with Old Bill, and Bairnsfather's cartoons became immensely popular. Some of them were made into postcards and sent as presents to men at the front. Later, books, plays, and even films were made about Old Bill.

In World War II, two American cartoon characters, known as Willie and Joe, represented ordinary US soldiers. The two downtrodden **GIs** were created by Bill Mauldin, who fought as a sergeant in North Africa. Mauldin's cartoons were published in *Stars and Stripes* magazine, which was read at home and by the troops abroad. Will and Joe are shown struggling through their daily lives in the army. Their humour helped to keep up the spirits of many real soldiers.

Filming wars

Ever since the cinematic camera was invented in the 1890s, it has been used to record conflicts and wars. Some of the earliest war documentaries were produced by the British Pathé News company. During the two World Wars, Pathé produced regular reports from the battlefront and these reports were screened in cinemas around the world.

At first, these silent black-and-white films were accompanied by captions, but by the time of World War II a spoken commentary and music were added.

Today, the tradition of recording wars continues. Now, the way that we receive news is far more immediate. Reporters and camera crew send digital images from the front lines, where they are often amongst the troops. This is dangerous work, and journalists can be killed s they try to record history as it is made. We can see their images via our televisions, newspapers, and mobile phones.

War in the movies

Ciné cameras were also used to create fictional images of war. In 1925, the great Russian director Sergei Eisenstein released the silent film *The Battleship Potemkin*. This very early war movie shocked its audience with its graphic scenes of an advancing army destroying everything in its path. The Hollywood studios were slower to concentrate on war, but following World War II, they produced dozens of war adventure stories. The Vietnam War was the subject of a number of dramatic films, including *Apocalypse Now* and *Full Metal Jacket*. These were very different to the World War II films that glorified war. In recent years, war films have included *Schindler's List, Pearl Harbor,* and *Saving Private Ryan*.

War music

Since the time of the earliest civilizations, people have used rousing music to prepare warriors for war and to help them march into battle.

Music for warriors

In many societies, warriors perform a ritual dance before they go to war. These dances are accompanied by music with a powerful, rhythmic beat. There is evidence of warriors playing war music in many ancient cultures. Archaeologists have found evidence that the Maya people of Mexico got in the mood for battle by playing music.

They shook rattles, beat ceramic (clay) drums, blew on conch shells, and beat turtle shells with deer antlers.

Each culture has its own instruments of war. The ancient Celts terrified their enemies by blowing on tall war trumpets. By the end of the Middle Ages, the descendants of the Celts in Scotland were playing bagpipes as they marched to war. Military bands today usually include drums, trumpets, bugles, and cymbals – all designed to make a rousing, rhythmic sound.

The United States Marine Corps military band. Bands like this play loud, rhythmic music to help soldiers keep in step. The cheerful music of military bands also helps to keep the soldiers spirits up when they are marching to war.

Illarion Pryanishnikov, *In the Year of 1812* (1874). This Russian painting shows the French army retreating after their defeat by the Russians. The Russian composer Tchaikovsky represented this Russian victory in his *1812 Overture*.

Marching songs

Even when soldiers have no instruments to play, they still sing songs to help them march in time. Some of the best-known marching songs in recent history were sung by the troops in World War One. British soldiers marching to the trenches tried to keep their spirits up by singing cheerful songs with titles such as "Pack up your troubles in your old kit bag and smile, smile, smile".

Describing war

Some composers have written music that tries to suggest the sounds and emotions of war. Beethoven's third symphony, known as the *Eroica*, was originally dedicated to the Emperor Napoleon. In its strong, stirring passages, it conveys the feeling of victory in battle. The Russian composer Tchaikovsky wrote his *1812 Overture* to represent Napoleon's defeat by the Russian army in 1812.

The overture includes marching tunes for the French and Russian armies and ends with a triumphant burst of sound, including real cannon fire. This dramatic conclusion marks the defeat of the French army, and expresses victory and new hope for Russia. Benjamin Britten's *War Requiem* commemorates the dead of World War II. It is a solemn, haunting work, expressing the sadness and loss of war.

Voices of protest

Many musicians have written songs protesting against war. The American Bob Dylan is a leading anti-war musician. Dylan started his long singing career in the 1960s and many of his songs were written as a protest against the war in Vietnam. His most famous anti-war songs are *Masters of War* and *Blowin' in the Wind*.

Stories, plays, and poems

Throughout time, people have told stories about war. At first these stories of heroes and their battles were recited or sung. People learnt the stories by heart and passed them down through the generations. Eventually, the stories and legends of war were written down by poets, or turned into plays.

Some of the earliest surviving stories of war come from Ancient India. The *Ramayana* and the *Mahabharata* were written down around the 3rd century BCE. These two long poems describe many conflicts between the **Hindu** gods, and between rival families. They are filled with gory battle scenes and have provided a rich source of inspiration for artists.

Novels of war

Some great novelists have written about war and conflict. In *A Tale of Two Cities,* Charles Dickens sets his story of love and sacrifice against the violent background of the French Revolution. Ernest Hemingway's novel *For whom the Bell Tolls* is a moving tale of heroism in the Spanish Civil War. Perhaps the most famous war novel ever written was Leo Tolstoy's *War and Peace.* This massive work covers the Napoleonic war in Russia in great detail. It contains vivid descriptions of battle, and clearly criticizes the pointless violence of war.

The theatre of war

War is the subject of many famous plays. William Shakespeare's play *Henry V* contains a rousing battle speech, delivered by the young King Harry as his troops prepare to fight the Battle of Agincourt. In contrast, Bertolt Brecht's play *Mother Courage and her Children* is a fierce attack on war. It was written in Germany in 1939, just as World War II was about to begin. In his powerful drama, which is set in the Thirty Years War of the 17th century, Brecht shows a family torn apart by conflict.

The poet's voice

Perhaps the most personal descriptions of war are found in poems. In particular, the young poets of World War I spoke very directly about their experiences. One of the most famous of these soldier poets is Wilfred Owen, who was killed in 1918. Owen's poems describe the agony of being gassed and of seeing his companions die. His poems also express his anger at the generals and politicians who sent thousands of young soldiers to a wasteful death.

William Shakespeare's play *Henry V* was made into a classic film, starring Sir Lawrence Olivier. Here, the young Henry gives a rousing speech to encourage his troops before the Battle of Agincourt.

The pity of war

In 1918 the war poet Wilfred Owen wrote, "I am not concerned with Poetry. My subject is War, and the pity of War. The Poetry is in the pity... All a poet can do today is warn. That is why the true Poets must be truthful."

Visions of peace

An ideal vision of a world where there is no war features in many people's minds. Some artists try and capture how such a paradise may look, sometimes referring to religious beliefs about peace.

The peaceable kingdom

Edward Hicks was an American artist who lived between 1780 and 1849. At this time there were many wars across the world. There was also conflict in America between the settlers from Europe and the Native Americans.

Hicks was a Quaker. Quakers are a religious group who believe that all conflict is wrong. He expressed his Quaker beliefs through his simple but effective paintings. Hicks produced a series of works with a theme of peace.

He created a peaceful kingdom where all the creatures live together in harmony. At the centre of his group of animals, Hicks always shows a young child. The figure of the loving child shows the artist's belief that it is possible for human beings to live peacefully. If only they are not taught to fight each other, they can remain all their lives like innocent, loving children.

Many of Hicks' animal paintings also feature a group of early settlers led by William Penn, the famous Quaker leader who founded the state of Pennsylvania. The paintings show Penn and his followers talking peacefully with the Native Americans. Hicks presented this scene of harmony as an example to his fellow settlers.

Edward Hicks, *The Peaceable Kingdom* (c.1833). In this vision of a perfect world, all creatures live in harmony. In the background, a group of settlers are holding a peaceful meeting with some Native Americans.

A place of peace

In 1971, John Lennon wrote his famous song *Imagine*, which presents a vision of a world without war. In this haunting song Lennon asks us to imagine a world where there are "no countries", "no religion", and "no possessions", which means that there is "nothing to kill or die for". In Lennon's perfect, imaginary world there are simply people "living life in peace" and "sharing all the world". *Imagine* was a massive hit all over the world. Over 30 years after it was written, it is still played at meetings and marches for peace.

The dove of peace

Although Christians have adopted the white dove to symbolize the Holy spirit, the dove is recognized by people all over the world as a symbol of peace and harmony.

Pablo Picasso's simple but forceful image of a dove flying with an olive branch in its beak has been used on flags, banners, and badges. For many people, it represents the hope of world peace.

In this image Picasso places the dove on a broken sword holding an olive branch in its beak, also a symbol of peace. Can you think of other occasions where the colour white is used as a sign of peace or harmony?

Map and Further reading

GERMANY
HOLLAND
UNITED KINGDOM
RUSSIA
EUROPE
FRANCE
ASIA
UNITED STATES OF AMERICA
ITALY
CHINA
JAPAN
SPAIN
GREECE
Atlantic Ocean
IRAN
Pacific Ocean
MEXICO
AFRICA
Pacific Ocean
SOUTH AMERICA
Indian Ocean
AUSTRALASIA

Map of the world

This map shows you roughly where in the world some key works of art mentioned in this book were produced. The countries marked on the map relate to entries in the timeline, opposite.

Further reading

History in Art series
(Raintree, 2005)

Directions in Art series
(Heinemann Library, 2003)

Art in History series
(Heinemann Library, 2001)

Eyewitness Art: Looking at Paintings, Jude Welton, (Dorling Kindersley, 1994)

Timeline

This timeline provides dates for some key works of art. Many of these dates are approximate, and are simply intended to give a rough idea of when the works were produced. You can see the relevant areas marked on the map of the world, opposite.

BCE

c.2500 The Royal Standard of Ur shows the Ancient Sumerian army in battle (modern-day Iran)

1400s Ancient Egyptian artists show pharaohs and warriors at war

400s Ancient Greek artists and sculptors start to glorify military heroes

c.200 The tomb of China's first emperor is filled with terracotta warriors

100s The Romans start to build monuments celebrating battle victories

Mayan artists start to show knights in battle (modern-day Mexico)

CE

800s Arab metal workers start to fashion fine weapons

c.1070 The *Bayeux Tapestry* is completed (France)

1100s Artists and writers in medieval Europe begin to create images and stories of knights

c.1440 Paolo Uccello paints three scenes from the battle of San Romano (Italy)

1600s Dutch artists produce large-scale paintings of battles at sea

1800s The tradition of painting samurai warriors flourishes in Japan

1800 Jacques-Louis David paints *Napoleon Crossing the Alps* (France)

1810 Francisco de Goya begins to produce his print series *Disasters of War* (Spain)

1812 Théodore Géricault paints *An Officer of the Hussars* (France)

1814 Goya paints *The Executions of the Third of May, 1808* (Spain)

1861 Mathew Brady begins to photograph the American Civil War

1865 Leo Tolstoy publishes *War and Peace* (Russia)

1916 Wilfred Owen starts to write war poems (UK)

1918 John Singer Sargent paints *Gassed* (USA)

1920s Käthe Kollwitz creates her series of *Woodcuts of War* (Germany)

1925 Sergei Eisenstein directs *The Battleship Potemkin* (Russia)

1937 Pablo Picasso paints *Guernica* (Spain)

1960s Bob Dylan composes and sings anti-war songs (USA)

1993 Steven Spielberg directs *Schindler's List* (USA)

Glossary

abstract showing an idea rather than a thing

aggression threatening or war-like behaviour

American Civil War a war between the northern and southern states of America that was fought from 1861 to 1865

ancestor a family member who lived a long time ago

Arabs a race of people who live in the Middle East or who come originally from the Middle East

archaeologist someone who studies the past by uncovering old objects or buildings and examining them carefully

Aztecs a warlike people who lived in Mexico from around 1300 to 1500

braves Native American warriors

campaign a series of attacks organized over a period of time in order to win a war

cannon a large, heavy gun on wheels

carnage the killing of a large number of people, especially in battle

chain-mail a kind of body armour made from linked metal rings

ciné a type of camera used for filming moving images

civil war war between different groups from the same country or area

civilian someone who is not a soldier and does not fight in wars

coat of arms a design in the shape of a shield that is used as the special sign of a family

codex/codices hand-made book/s

commission to pay an artist to create a work of art

corpse dead body

depict/depicting to show something or somebody in a work of art

favour a strong liking for somebody

formal proper and not casual

fresco a wall painting

general an important army commander, in charge of hundreds of soldiers

geometric using forms found in geometry, such as a square, a triangle, and a circle

GI an ordinary soldier in the American army

Hindu a follower of Hinduism, the main religion and culture of India and Nepal

illuminated illustrated with painted patterns and pictures

indigenous belonging to the first people to live in a place or a country

Islamic the civilization developed by Muslims, who follow the religion Islam

joust a practice battle

knight a skilled warrior. In medieval Europe, knights rode on horses.

loincloth a simple cloth worn around the waist and hips

manuscript a hand-written book

Maori the first people to settle in New Zealand. The Maoris arrived in New Zealand around 750 CE.

maritime connected with the sea

massacre a brutal killing of large numbers of people

medieval belonging to the period from approximately 1000 CE to 1450 CE

Middle Ages the period of history between approximately 1000–1450 CE

mosaic a picture or pattern made up of tiny pieces of coloured stone or glass

mural a painting on a wall

musket a large old-fashioned gun

napalm jellied form of petrol that can stick to the skin and cause extensive burns

Nazi party a party led by Adolf Hitler, who ruled Germany between 1933 and 1945. The Nazis used force against anyone who disagreed with them.

pharaoh an Ancient Egyptian ruler

pigment paint made from natural materials such as earth

porcupine a small animal with very long spikes (or quills) on its back

portrait an artwork, such as a painting, that represents a person

prehistoric belonging to a time millions of years ago, before history was written down

print a picture made by covering a carved design with ink and then printing the design onto paper

pyramid a structure that has a flat, square base and sloping, triangular sides forming a point at the top

quillwork designs made from porcupine quills (or spikes)

ransom money that is demanded before someone can be set free

Republicans a group in the Spanish Civil War who fought against General Franco to keep their country free

romantic passionate and full of feeling

Romantics a group of artists and writers who concentrated on showing feelings and emotions. The Romantic Movement began in the late 18th century and flourished in the early 19th century.

sacred holy

samurai a Japanese warrior

sculptor someone who makes works of art from stone, wood, metal, or other materials

sculpture a work of art made from stone, wood, metal, or other materials

tapestry a heavy piece of cloth with pictures or patterns woven into it

tattoo to use needles and ink or natural pigments in order to print a design on somebody's skin

tournament an event held in medieval times, in which knights practised their battle skills by taking part in jousts and other contests

Union army the army of the northern states in the American Civil War

watercolour a type of painting, using paints that can be mixed with water

Yankees the name given to the people of the northern states in the American Civil War

Index

African peoples 14-15
Alexander the Great 10, 11
American Civil War 32-33
Arab warriors 22
armies 6-9
armour 8, 10, 18, 20, 22
atomic bomb 37
Augustus 12
Aztecs 16

Bairnsfather, Bruce 44-45
battle scenes 26-29
Bayeux Tapestry 18, 19
Beethoven, Ludwig van 47
body painting 15
Brady, Mathew 33, 39
Braque, Georges 41
Brecht, Bertolt 48
Britten, Benjamin 47

Capa, Robert 39
cartoons 42, 44-45
Catlin, George 25
Celts 46
chain-mail 18
Chapman, Jake and Dinos 31
China 8
civilians 38-41
codices 16, 17
costumes 14, 16, 24
counting coup 25
Crimean War 42
Cubism 41

dances, ceremonial 14, 15, 46
David, Jacques-Louis 28
Delacroix, Eugéne 28-29
Dickens, Charles 48
duels 22, 23
Dylan, Bob 47

Egypt, Ancient 7

featherwork 16, 24

films and documentaries 37, 45
Flagg, Montmorency 42

Géricault, Théodore 4
Gérôme, Jean-Léon 23
Goya, Francisco 30-31
Greece, Ancient 10-11
Guernica 40-41

headdresses 10, 14, 15, 16, 22, 24
Hemingway, Ernest 48
heraldry 21
Hicks, Edward 50
Homer, Winslow 32
Hope, Captain James 33
horses 4, 18, 22, 28

Iliad 11
illuminations 18
India 48

Japan 8, 22
jousts 20-21

King Arthur and the Round Table 18
knights 16, 18, 20-21, 22, 26
Kollwitz, Käthe 31, 38-39

Lambert, George 34
Lennon, John 51
Leutze, Emanuel Gottlieb 29

manuscripts 18, 21
Maori warriors 15
marching songs 47
maritime paintings 27
masks 14, 22
Mauldin, Bill 45
Maya 16, 46
metalwork 20, 22
Middle Ages 18-21, 23, 28, 46
monuments 12, 13
Moore, Henry 36

mosaics 10, 11
murals 40-41
music 46-47

Napoleon Bonaparte 4, 13, 28, 30, 47
Nash, Paul 36
Native Americans 24-25, 50
Nevinson, Christopher 34
Norman Conquest 18
novels, stories, and plays 23, 48, 49

Owen, Wilfred 48

pain and suffering 31, 35, 38-41
Paton, Joseph 42
peace 50-51
pharaohs 7
photography 5, 33, 34, 37, 39
photojournalism 39
Picasso, Pablo 31, 40-41, 51
poetry 48
posters 42-43
protest songs 47
Pryanishnikov, Illarion 47

Quakers 50
quillwork 24

realism 30, 31, 32, 33
Romans 12-13
Romantic Movement 28-29, 30

samurai 8, 22, 23
Sargent, John Singer 35
sculpture 10, 12, 13, 16
Shakespeare, William 23, 48
shoguns 22
soldiers, warriors 7-25, 26, 32-33, 34, 35, 44-45
Spanish Civil War 39, 40-1, 48

Spencer, Stanley 34
Standard of Ur 6
Sumeria 6

tattoos 15
Tchaikovsky, Piotr Ilyich 47
terracotta warriors 8, 9
Tolstoy, Leo 48
tomb figures 8
tournaments 20-21
Trajan's Column 13

Uccello, Paolo 26
Ut, Nic 39

van Wieringen, Cornelis Claesz 27
victory columns and arches 13
Vietnam War 39, 45, 47

Washington, George 29
weapons 7, 8, 11, 14, 18, 20, 22
women and children 38-39, 42
World War I 34-35, 38, 42, 44-45, 47, 48
World War II 36-37, 42, 45, 48